T0352903

Millie Marotta's

Tropical
Wonderland

First published in the United Kingdom in 2020 by
Batsford
43 Great Ormond Street
London WC1N 3HZ

An imprint of B. T. Batsford Holdings Limited

Illustrations copyright © Millie Marotta 2015
Volume copyright © B. T. Batsford Ltd 2020

The moral rights of the author have been asserted.

All rights reserved. No part of this publication may be reproduced, stored in a retrieval system,
or transmitted in any form or by any means, electronic, mechanical, photocopying, recording or
otherwise, without the prior written permission of the copyright owner.

ISBN 978 1 84994 591 2

A CIP catalogue record for this book is available from the
British Library.

20 19 18 17 16 15 14 13 12 11 10 9 8 7
30 29 28 27 26 25 24

Reproduction by Mission Productions Ltd, Hong Kong
Printed and bound by Toppan Leefung Printing Ltd, China

Millie Marotta's
Tropical Wonderland

pocket colouring

BATSFORD

Introduction

Those of you who already own my first colouring book *Animal Kingdom* will know that my favourite things in life are drawing and the natural world – a match made in heaven in my opinion. Like *Animal Kingdom*, this book forms a collection of illustrations of flora and fauna, this time inspired by my own travels to far-flung places and all the exotic species that I have been lucky enough to see along the way. It also includes some of those that I've not yet been fortunate enough to see for myself in the wild, and so in that sense it also serves to satisfy my own flight of fancy and general obsession with nature. My illustrations always begin as fairly realistic drawings, keeping the overall form of the animal or plant quite true to life. I will then begin to elaborate and decorate, adding lots of pattern and detail to create something which is part real and part imagination.

Putting together the first book was both a new and exciting experience for me. As a commercial illustrator I was of course used to having my work out there in the public eye, but had never offered it to people in a way that they were being invited to contribute to the artwork themselves. I did feel a little nervous about how the book might be received – would people enjoy colouring my illustrations? Would they be charmed, as I was hoping, by my own interpretation of the animal kingdom? As it turns out the response to the book has been overwhelmingly positive and it has been a joy to share my work in this way with so many people.

I have discovered too that many readers felt they were getting a lot more from the book than just a creative activity. Many have been in touch explaining how the book has helped them in some way through difficult times and has served as a form of 'art therapy' for them. As someone who has always enjoyed drawing, painting and doodling, I have always appreciated how therapeutic these types of creative activities can be and have been lucky enough that they have been a regular and important part of my life for as far back as I can remember. So to know that *Animal Kingdom* has been so much more than just a colouring book to many readers is wonderful.

It has been utterly fascinating to see how inventive readers are with their colouring and how they can transform a black and white illustration created by me into something completely unique and very much their own. With *Tropical Wonderland* I simply wanted to do the same thing again – to delight people with beautiful illustrations and inspire them to want to explore their creative side. And to offer a little bit of escapism.

Although *Tropical Wonderland* is predominantly a colouring book, you will find a few pages dotted throughout with empty spaces, inviting you to embellish them with your own patterns, textures and drawings.

A question I have been asked a lot since the release of *Animal Kingdom* is which I prefer myself for colouring – pens or pencils. I have to say that for me it will always be coloured pencils, because I enjoy how versatile they are in allowing for shading and colour blending, but that is just my personal preference.

I think the most interesting thing for me is seeing how differently readers will approach the same image in terms of the colours and materials they choose, resulting in strikingly individual outcomes. While one person may go for a very calming harmonious palette in soft pencils, the next might choose a selection of lively vibrant colours that clash with one another, but each will achieve a great result. I guess what I'm saying here is that there are no rules – you will all begin with the same illustrations but your choice of colours is just that – your choice. It is this that will make the images in your book uniquely yours, there is no right or wrong way to colour, just go with what you feel and create a tropical wonderland all of your own.

Millie Marotta

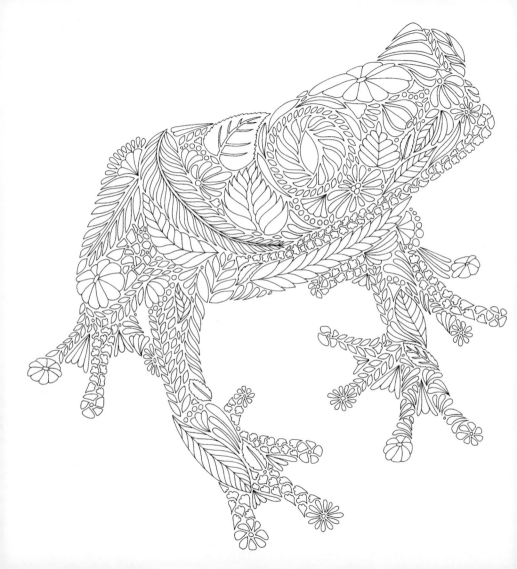

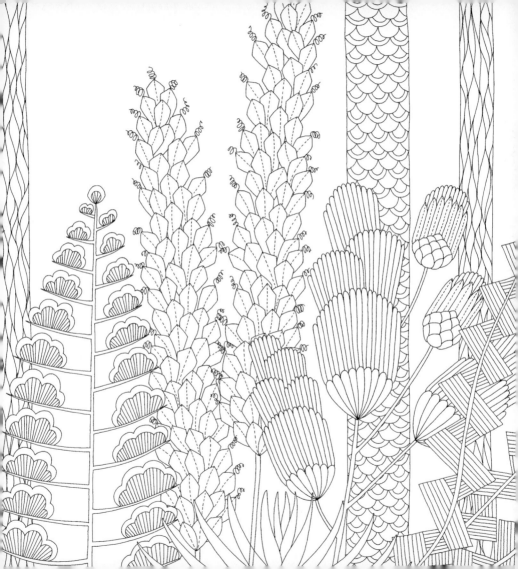

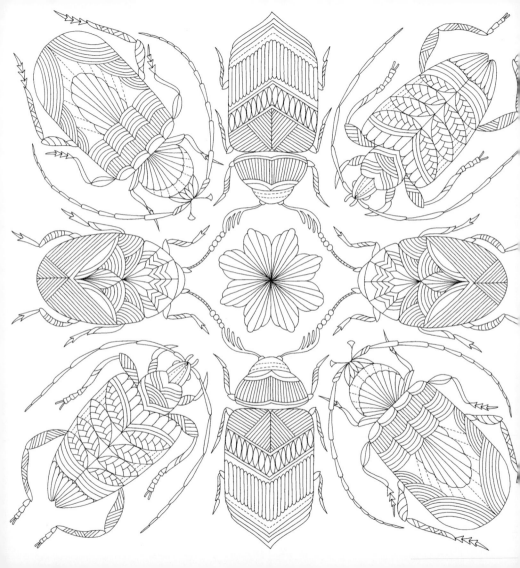

List of creatures in *Tropical Wonderland*

For those of you who are curious to know, here's
a list of the illustrations, in the order that they
appear in the book.

Tropical flowers

Pineapple

Flamingos

Screech owl

Butterfly and shield bugs

Toucan

Ring-tailed lemur

Corals and sponges

Jellyfish

Macaws

Floral pattern

Floral round

Cockatoos

Leopard

Tropical butterflies

Tamarin monkey

Fruit bats

Passion flower

Discus fish

Hornbill

Banded pittas

Spider monkeys

Hummingbirds

Tropical bird in nest

Tropical plants

Roseate spoonbill

Berries, buds, leaves and seeds

Indian elephants

Tree frog

Iguana

Tropical plants and trees

Tropical blooms

Luna moth

Ibis

Tropical insects

Peacock

Rainforest leaves

Seahorses

Moon crab

Grasshopper

Lilies and lily pads

Tropical feathers

Victoria crowned pigeon

Tropical blooms, leaves and seed-heads

Baboon

Margay

Vines and blossoms

Jewel beetles

Swallowtail butterfly

Tropical florals

Cacti

Elephant

Toadstools and mushrooms

Grey crowned crane

Rufous fantails

Tropical bugs

Green turtle

Poison dart frogs

Tropical birds

Bush baby

Armadillo

Screech owl

Angelfish

Create your own tropical wonderland here...

Test your colour palettes…